# MONSTER FIGHT CLUB
# GODS AND GODDESSES

## ANITA GANERI AND DAVID WEST

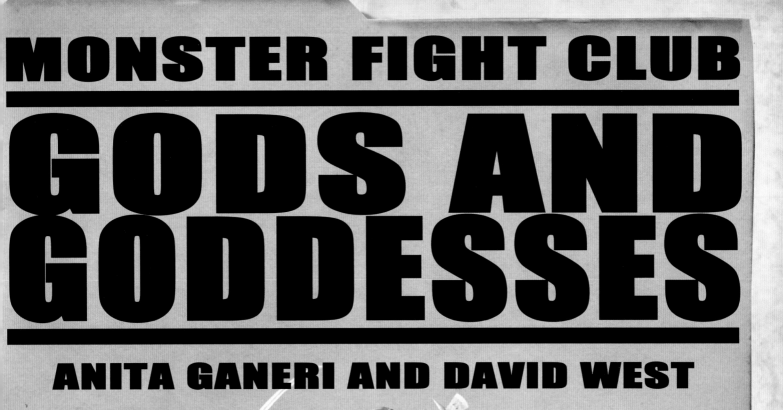

**PowerKiDS** press

New York

Published in 2012 by The Rosen Publishing Group, Inc.
29 East 21st Street, New York, NY 10010

*Designed and produced by*
David West Books

*Designer and illustrator:* David West
*Editor:* Ronne Randall
*U.S. Editor:* Kara Murray

Library of Congress Cataloging-in-Publication Data
Ganeri, Anita, 1961–
Gods and goddesses / By Anita Ganeri.
p. cm. — (Monster fight club)
Includes index.
ISBN 978-1-4488-5202-4 (library binding) — ISBN 978-1-4488-5242-0 (pbk.) —
ISBN 978-1-4488-5243-7 (6-pack)
1. Gods—Juvenile literature. 2. Goddesses—Juvenile literature. I. Title.
BL473.G28 2012
398.21—dc22

2011002913

Manufactured in China

CPSIA Compliance Information: Batch #DS1102PK:
For Further Information contact Rosen Publishing, New York,
New York at 1-800-237-9932

# CONTENTS

# INTRODUCTION

Welcome to the Monster Fight Club! Watch in awe as gods and goddesses from myth and legend enter the ring to do battle. Have you ever wondered who would win—mighty Odin or all-powerful Zeus? Find out as you enter their weird and wonderful world.

## How Does It Work?

There are six monster fights in this book. Before each fight, you will see a profile page for each contestant. These pages give you more information about them. Once you have read the profile pages, you might be able to take a better guess at who will win the fight.

*The profile pages are crammed with fascinating and bloodcurdling facts about each of the contestants.*

## WARNING

Blood will be spilled!

*The illustrations show the contestants in some of their other gory guises.*

PROFILE: **HADES**

A snarling beast, fleet of foot, cunning as a fox, and boasting huge claws, a muzzle full of foul teeth, and supernatural strength, you will only see a werewolf during a full moon. Something they have in common with lunatics.

### One of the Three
Common methods include sleeping outdoors during a full moon, being born under a full moon, drinking from the water in a wolf's footprint, and being cursed. Lycanthropy (the transformation of a human into a wolf).

### Character Traits
In human form werewolves are believed to have some strange, suspiciously wolf-like features. These include pale, rough skin, bushy eyebrows that grow to meet in the middle, hair on the face, hands and feet, pointed ears, and long, red fingernails shaped like almonds. ears, and long, red fingernails shaped like almonds.

*To get to Hades, the soles of the dead paid the ferryman to cross the River Styx.*

*Hades sometimes had a softside. He allowed Orpheus to take his dead wife back so long as he didn't turn round to look at her which of course he did.*

*Hades is often shown with the three-headed dog, Cerberus who guards the gates of Hades.*

10

PROFILE: **MICTLANTECUHTLI**

A vampire is a member of the living dead. This blood-sucker wakes up at night, leaving its coffin to hunt for humans. It drinks their blood in order to carry on its evil existence. It hunts in human form, or as an animal, and must return to its resting place before daybreak. It has been known since ancient times, but most vampire folklore comes from 18th-century Eastern Europe.

*Mictlantecuhtli eating a dead sole from a Codex.*

### Where in the Underworld?
The typical vampire has a mesmerizing face, with bright, clear eyes, eyebrows that meet in the middle, and an open mouth revealing fangs. Sometimes blood drips from the corner of its mouth. Vampires also have long fingernails and are quite thin and pale with the look of a dead person due to a lack of blood.

### Character Traits
Anybody bitten by a vampire was thought to become a vampire after death. Anybody bitten by a vampire was thought to become a vampire after. Anybody bitten by a vampire was thought to become a vampire after death. Anybody bitten by a vampire was thought to become a

*Mictlantecuhtli was an important god in the Aztec pantheon especially when multi-human sacrifices were common as shown in the Codex Magliabechiano.*

*Ceramic statue of Mictlantecuhtli recovered during excavations of the House of Eagles in the Templo Mayor.*

*In this modern depiction, Mictlantecuhtli is shown carrying the obsidian edged weapon of an Aztec warrior.*

11

*These large illustrations show you each contestant, warts and all, to give you a good idea of their physical features.*

*In the main text, read a chilling account of how each fight progresses.*

*Each of the contestants may also fight under a different name, shown here as AKA (Also Known As).*

# FIGHT 2: HADES VS MICTLANTECUHTLI

**M**eeting in the underworld these two terrible gods approach each other with mistaken preconceptions. Hades thinks he is dealing with a nutcase who has come to steal souls from his kingdom which send him into a rage. Mictlantecuhtli sees the man with the dog as a reluctant sole who needs to be educated in the ways of the dead. Hades unleashes his dog who is delighted

at the prospect of so many bones. The snarling beast sends the Aztec god scuttling up onto a rock ledge. As each cannot speak the others language the confusion continues as Hades dons his Helm of darkness and becomes invisible. Hades creeps up on the Aztec and kicks him off the ledge where the waiting Cerberus gets stuck in. The dog runs off with two leg bones and an arm bone which puts the Lord of Mictlan at a distinct disadvantage. The fight ends with Hades dragging off Mictlantecuhtli to Tartarus where the Aztec finds himself quite at home.

The vampire is unhurt and in the instant the werewolf is on him it has changed into a bat and flown out of the werewolf's reach. The werewolf stumbles as it avoids a patch of wolfsbane growing by a tombstone. The bat swoops upon the werewolf from behind. The werewolf's senses picks up the bat's movements and it twists round and strikes the bat with its clawed hands. Again the vampire recovers.

Dawn is approaching and as the first weak rays of light appear the werewolf begins to lose its powers and it starts to morph back to its human form. The vampire is unhurt and in the instant the

**STATS**
## HADES
AKA Pluto, God of the Underworld

**STRENGTHS:** Can become in visible when he wears the Helm of Darkness. Has a terrible anger. Has a vicious dog with three heads. He is a god so can not be killed.

**WEAKNESSES:** Can be persuaded to be kind.

**STATS**
## MICTLANTECUHTLI
AKA Lord of Mictlan, Aztec God of the Dead

**STRENGTHS:** Very scary. Ready to tear anybody apart. Collects eyeballs to make into necklaces. Difficult to kill as he is already dead.

**WEAKNESSES:** All skin and bones. Can be tricked.

**WINNER: HADES**

12

13

*At-a-glance STATS boxes give you vital information about each of the contestants, including their main strengths and weaknesses.*

*The winner's name is given in this black box in the right-hand corner. Of course, you might not agree.*

## The Monster Fight
After reading the profile pages for each contestant, turn the page to see the fight. Check out the STATS (Statistics) boxes, which give details of the fighters' main strengths and weaknesses. Then read a blow-by-blow account of the battle—if you dare. The winner, if there is one, is shown in a small black box in the bottom right-hand corner.

# PROFILE: **ODIN**

From his throne in Asgard, Odin, king of the Norse gods, kept watch over the nine worlds. God of war, mighty Odin was also wise, sacrificing one of his eyes to drink from the fountain of knowledge. He often left Asgard in disguise to visit the world of humans.

*Odin sacrificed one eye for a drink from the fountain of knowledge.*

## Hall of the Slain

Valhalla, the Hall of the Slain, was Odin's magnificent hall in Asgard. This was where the Valkyries, Odin's female warrior-servants, brought the bravest of the warriors who had been slain in battle to feast and fight.

## Future Death

According to Norse mythology, there will be a great final battle, called Ragnarok, between the forces of good (the gods) and evil (the giants and monsters). At this battle, many of the gods will die, including Odin, who will be killed by the wolf Fenrir.

*At Ragnarok, Odin will be killed by the giant wolf Fenrir.*

*Odin rode on an eight-legged horse, called Sleipnir, accompanied by two wolves.*

# PROFILE: **ZEUS**

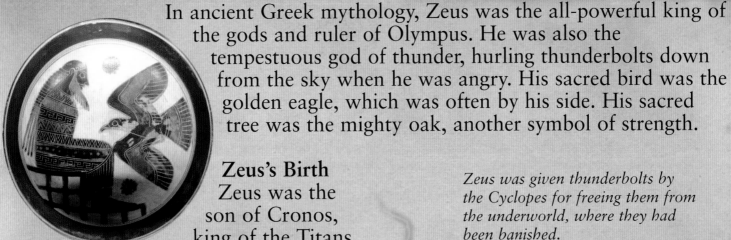

In ancient Greek mythology, Zeus was the all-powerful king of the gods and ruler of Olympus. He was also the tempestuous god of thunder, hurling thunderbolts down from the sky when he was angry. His sacred bird was the golden eagle, which was often by his side. His sacred tree was the mighty oak, another symbol of strength.

*Zeus is often shown with an eagle by his side.*

### Zeus's Birth

Zeus was the son of Cronos, king of the Titans, and his wife, Rhea. Cronos had been warned that one of his children would kill him, so he swallowed each as it was born. To save Zeus, Rhea tricked Cronos into swallowing a stone and gave Zeus to a nymph to raise.

*Zeus was given thunderbolts by the Cyclopes for freeing them from the underworld, where they had been banished.*

## Zeus and Hera

Zeus was married to the goddess Hera, and they had several children. But he also had affairs with other women, many of them mortal. Hera grew jealous of her husband's behavior and tried to stop him. To distract her, Zeus sent a nymph named Echo, who talked to Hera nonstop. As punishment, Hera condemned Echo to repeating the last words that other people said.

*Zeus often appeared on Earth in disguise. Once, he appeared as a white bull to Princess Europa, whom he carried off to the island of Crete.*

# FIGHT 1: ODIN VS. ZEUS

Taking part in tonight's first fight are two of the greatest gods of mythology—the warlike Odin and the temperamental Zeus. Both fearless, all-powerful, and master shape-shifters, they have, in a peculiar quirk of history, come out of retirement to compete for the role of supreme deity.

Odin rides out of Valhalla on his eight-legged horse, Sleipnir, with two faithful wolves. As ever, two ravens, black as night, swoop around his shoulders, bringing back reports of what is happening in the world.

## STATS
## ODIN
AKA Wodin, One-eyed, Allfather

**STRENGTHS:** Starts wars by throwing Gungnir, a magical spear that never misses its target. Cunning, and can shape-shift into any animal. Has two spies in the form of ravens.

**WEAKNESSES:** Has only one eye (sacrificed the other to gain wisdom).

# ZEUS

AKA Jupiter (Roman), Zeus Olympios, Zeus Panhellenios

**STRENGTHS:** Immortal and all-powerful. Rules the Earth with his brothers, Poseidon and Hades. Uses thunderbolts as weapons.

**WEAKNESSES:** Likes visiting the Earth and getting involved in mortal affairs. Terrifying when angry.

Meanwhile, from his vantage point on Mount Olympus, the great Zeus stands alone, watching Odin's progress and choosing his moment to strike…

Seeing Zeus, Odin lets fly with Gungnir, his magical spear made by the dwarves, which never misses its target. True to form, the spear hits its target dead center—and bounces off!

Furious, Zeus hurls down a thunderbolt. It narrowly misses Odin but catches one of the ravens, which disappears in a cloud of smoke and feathers.

Odin is stunned by Zeus's power. As a mighty god of war, he is not used to being crossed in battle. As he prepares to throw Gungnir again, he sends his remaining raven back to Valhalla to summon the Valkyries to his side. But Zeus is also growing frustrated—his trusty thunderbolts have still not touched Odin.

And so the fight continues, but ultimately reaches a stalemate. For this is a battle that neither of these great gods can win. Zeus is immortal and cannot be killed by Gungnir or any other weapon. Odin will only be killed at Ragnarok, the last great battle between the gods and the giants, which is still to come. The only possible result is a draw.

# DRAW

# PROFILE: **HADES**

The ancient Greek god of the underworld, Hades was said to have had a fearsome personality and ruled over the gloomy home of the dead. He rode a chariot pulled by four black horses. To the living, his reputation was so terrifying that people dared not say his name.

## Three Brothers

Hades was the brother of Zeus and Poseidon. After defeating their father and the Titans in a fierce battle, Zeus became ruler of the sky, Poseidon king of the ocean, and Hades ruler of the underworld.

## Hades and Persephone

Hades' wife was Persephone, daughter of Demeter, goddess of plants. Hades kidnapped her and took her down to the underworld. Grief-stricken, Demeter set off to find her, leaving the plants and crops to die. Finally, Hades agreed that Persephone could spend part of each year with her mother. Then the plants bloom and it is spring.

*To cross the River Styx and enter the underworld the dead had to pay the ferryman Charon.*

*In one myth, Hades allowed Orpheus to take his dead wife back from the underworld, as long as he did not turn around to look at her—but he did.*

*Hades is often shown with Cerberus, a three-headed dog who guards the gates to the underworld.*

# PROFILE: **MICTLANTECUHTLI**

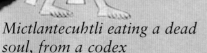

The terrifying lord of the dead in Aztec mythology, Mictlantecuhtli ruled Mictlan, the lowest level of the underworld. Traditionally shown as a skeleton with a skull-like head, he wore a necklace of human eyeballs and earplugs of human bones. He and his equally nightmarish wife lived in a windowless house in Mictlan and were associated with bats, owls and spiders.

*Mictlantecuhtli eating a dead soul, from a codex*

*A statue of Mictlantecuhtli, discovered during the excavation of Aztec ruins in Mexico City*

## Journey to Mictlan

To reach Mictlan, the souls of the dead had a long and dangerous journey through the nine levels of the underworld. There were many trials to go through, including crossing a river of blood, being blown by a knife-filled wind, and battling wild beasts. People were buried with food and items to help them on their way.

## Bone Thieves

In Aztec myth, the god of the wind, Quetzalcoatl, was sent to Mictlan to bring back the bones of the last people on Earth. These were needed to make human beings. Mictlantecuhtli tricked Quetzalcoatl into dropping the bones, and they shattered. But he picked up the pieces and managed to escape.

*Mictlantecuhtli was one of the most important Aztec gods. His worship often included human sacrifice, as shown in this image from an Aztec codex.*

*In this modern image, Mictlantecuhtli is shown carrying the obsidian-edged weapon of an Aztec warrior.*

# FIGHT 2: HADES VS. MICTLANTECUHTL

Deep down in the dreadful gloom of the underworld, two lords of death approach each other for a truly grisly showdown. In the far corner is Hades, guarded as ever by his ferocious, three-headed hound, Cerberus. Opposite him stands the sinister and skeletally thin figure of Mictlantecuhtli, eyes sunk deep into his skull, and armed with a weapon edged in razor-sharp obsidian.

## STATS
# HADES
### AKA Pluto (Roman)

**STRENGTHS:** Can become invisible when he wears the Helm of Darkness. A brave fighter. Immortal, so cannot be killed. Has a fierce, three-headed guard dog.

**WEAKNESSES:** Quick to anger. Can be persuaded to be kind.

Both of these gods are dangerous, and neither likes intruders. Believing that Mictlantecuhtli has come to steal souls from his kingdom, Hades flies into a terrible rage. He shouts an order at Cerberus, who has been straining at his leash. The terrifying beast leaps forward, ready to sink his teeth into Mictlantecuhtli but he is not quite quick enough. Mictlantecuhtli has ordered his demons to dig a deep pit right across the dog's path. When Cerberus pounces, the god unleashes a thick cloud of bats that fly into the dog's face, and he plunges into the pit.

Cackling wildly, Mictlantecuhtli retreats to a rocky ledge to get a good vantage point. With Cerberus gone, he can smell victory. But Hades isn't finished yet. Quick as a flash, he puts on the Helm of Darkness, a helmet created by the Cyclopes, which makes its wearer invisible. Mictlantecuhtli basks in his misplaced glory, while Hades creeps up beside him and pushes him off the ledge.

With a bloodcurdling shriek, Mictlantecuhtli plummets into a raging chasm of fire and flames. For a while Hades can hear an eerie howling, but then silence falls. For now, at least, Mictlantecuhtli is destroyed. But he is no ordinary enemy, and Hades knows that he will return.

## STATS

## MICTLANTECUHTLI
### AKA Lord of Mictlan

**STRENGTHS:** Terrifying appearance. Collects eyeballs to make into necklaces. Already dead, so difficult to kill.

**WEAKNESSES:** Skin and bone. Can be tricked.

**WINNER: HADES**

# PROFILE: **DURGA**

In Hindu mythology, Durga is a warlike goddess who was created by the gods from a beam of light. Her task was to fight the evil demons who threatened humankind. Durga's feats are celebrated every year at the great Durga Puja festival.

*Durga's weapons were given to her by the gods.*

## Many Weapons

Traditionally, Durga is shown with eight arms, each holding a different weapon. These weapons symbolize her powers and were given to her by the gods. She rides on a tiger, another symbol of her strength.

*Durga fighting the demon Mahishasura. He and his army had unleashed a reign of terror on the world, but the gods could not defeat him because he could only be killed by a woman.*

## Fighting the Demons

According to Hindu legend, a terrible demon, called Mahishasura, once terrorized the Earth. He could not be defeated by a man, so the gods created Durga to fight him. Seeing the goddess, Mahishasura turned into a giant buffalo and charged. But Durga was ready. She caught the buffalo in a lasso and cut off his head with her sword.

*Durga is often shown riding on a tiger or sometimes a lion.*

# PROFILE: THE MORRIGAN

The Morrigan is an Irish goddess. She sometimes appears as a woman with long, flowing hair, a long cloak, and a spear in her hand. But she can also appear as an animal—a crow, eel, or cow—changing her shape at will.

## Goddess of War

The Morrigan is a goddess of war and is often seen on battlefields. Legend says that her appearance foretells the death of a warrior. The Morrigan has many powers that can completely change the outcome of a battle. In one story, she recites a poem that brings a battle to an end and drives the enemy into the sea.

*The Morrigan sometimes shape-shifts into a crow and flies above warriors on a battlefield.*

## The Morrigan and Cuchulainn

There are many legends about the Morrigan's encounters with the hero and warrior Cuchulainn. In one story, the Morrigan offers to help Cuchulainn in battle, but he refuses. Insulted, she appears at his next battle, to cause trouble. First she appears as a cow and knocks him over. Then she appears as an eel and trips him. Next she appears as a wolf and grabs his sword arm. Despite this, he wins.

*A modern image of the Morrigan*

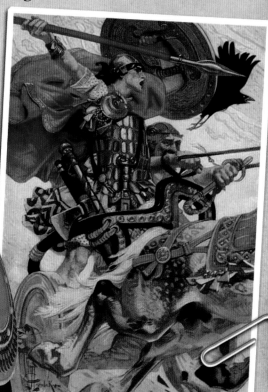

*One story tells how the Morrigan appears to Cuchulainn as an old woman, washing his armor in a stream. This is an omen of his death. Later, mortally wounded, he straps himself to a stone so that he can die upright. It is only when the Morrigan, in the shape of a crow, lands on his shoulder that his enemies believe he is truly dead.*

# FIGHT 3: DURGA VS. THE MORRIGAN

On tonight's bill are two fearsome goddesses of war. Both are powerful forces whose appearance on a battlefield is enough to strike fear into their enemies' hearts. First comes Durga, riding on a tiger, a weapon in each of her eight arms. Facing her is the Morrigan, armed only with a sword and shield, but ready to change shape at will.

## STATS
# DURGA
**AKA** Maa Durga

**STRENGTHS:** Has eight arms, so can hold eight weapons. Powerful laughter that triggers earthquakes. Rides a tiger.

**WEAKNESSES:** Does not like shape-shifters.

Immediately, the Morrigan tries to take control by suddenly shape-shifting into cow and charging at Durga. The tiger jumps back in shock, but Durga quickly eadies it and fends off the Morrigan with her sword and spear. Surprised at the erocity of her opponent's attack, the Morrigan backs off and goes on the defensive. ut Durga isn't fooled. She knows that the Morrigan has magical powers and can hange the outcome of a battle simply by chanting a spell. The tiger leaps at the Morrigan, its claws extended, while Durga prepares to cut off her head. All seems ost, but at the last minute the Morrigan changes into a crow and flies out of reach.

As the fight continues, Durga seems to have the upper hand. She has better eapons and is used to fighting against armies of demons. But the Morrigan isn't nished yet. In a flash, she changes into a wolf, which sinks its teeth into the tiger's eg. The tiger yelps in pain. Durga redoubles her attack until she has the Morrigan acked up against a cliff by a stream. There seems to be no way out. Durga laughs t the defenseless Morrigan, causing an earthquake, which dislodges an avalanche of ocks and buries the Irish goddess. Durga celebrates her victory, but nknown to her, the Morrigan has turned into an eel and wims away, ready to fight another day.

STATS

# THE MORRIGAN

AKA Morrigu, Morgan, Morrighan

**STRENGTHS:** Able to shape-shift into different animals. Has the gift of foretelling the future.

**WEAKNESSES:** Does not like being crossed or insulted. Bears a grudge.

**WINNER: DURGA**

# PROFILE: ANANSI

A very popular figure in African and West Indian folktales, Anansi is half man, half spider, famous for his cunning, trickery, and feats. There are many stories of Anansi outwitting his enemies, and many more that tell of his tricks backfiring on him.

## Spider Man

Legend says that Anansi was the son of Nyame, the sky god. His father turned him into a spider because of his mischief, though he is sometimes shown as a cross between human and spider. Small and slight, he often wins his battles through cunning rather than strength.

*The figure of Anansi is similar to other tricksters, such as Coyote or Raven, found in many Native American myths.*

## Stealing Wisdom

One day, Anansi decided to steal all the wisdom in the world. He found a pot and went from door to door, asking for wisdom and advice. Then he sealed the pot and looked for a tall tree to hide it in. But the pot was too heavy for him to carry, and he let it slip. It smashed on the ground and all the wisdom spread around the world, causing Anansi's plan to backfire.

*Treat spiders with care—one of them might be Anansi.*

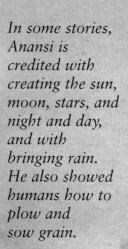

*In some stories, Anansi is credited with creating the sun, moon, stars, and night and day, and with bringing rain. He also showed humans how to plow and sow grain.*

*Anansi stories are best known in West Africa. They were passed on by word of mouth. Later, as the slave trade spread, they were taken to the West Indies.*

# PROFILE: **LOKI**

*Three of Loki's children—Fenrir, the wolf; Jormungand the serpent; and Hel, queen of the dead*

In Norse mythology, Loki was the son of two mighty fire giants and was blood brother to Odin. He lived with the gods in Asgard. Legend says that Loki was handsome, mischievous, and cunning. He was also a talented shape-shifter, able to change into any animal at will. At first these feats amused the gods, but later the gods began to turn against Loki.

## Loki's Brood

With the giantess Angrboda, Loki had three terrible children—Fenrir, the wolf; Jormungand, the serpent; and Hel, a monstrous daughter who became queen of the dead. His wife was the goddess Sigyn, and they had two sons—Vali and Narvi. Despite Loki's evil deeds, Sigyn always stood by him and tried to protect him.

## Punishment of Loki

The god Baldr was Odin's son. He was wise and loved by everyone except Loki. Loki tricked Baldr's brother, Hod, into killing Baldr then refused to help bring Baldr back to life. Furious, the gods decided Loki should be punished. They bound him to a rock underneath a snake that dripped deadly poison down on him.

*Loki's good relationship with the gods ended when he helped bring about the death of Baldr.*

*During Loki's punishment, Sigyn tried to save him by holding up a bowl that collected the snake's poison, but she could not stop drips from falling on Loki.*

*Loki the giant*

# FIGHT 4: ANANSI VS. LOKI

Being picked to fight Anansi is good news for Loki. It means that he has been released from his living misery of being tied to a rock while a snake drips poison onto him. His main aim in accepting the challenge is to escape the vengeance of the Norse gods. But if he can beat the trickster Anansi, so much the better. Whatever happens, it cannot be worse than his previous fate.

The two gods eye each other up carefully. Based on first appearances, Loki seems to have the upper hand. The son of giants, he is powerfully built and heavily armed. In contrast, Anansi is small and slight, with eight limbs but no weapons. But, as both contestants know, appearances can be deceptive.

STATS
## ANANSI
AKA Kwaku Ananse, Anancy, Aunt Nancy

STRENGTHS: Cunning and intelligent. Wins by guile, not strength. Can be a spider or a human.

WEAKNESSES: Small and slight. Has no weapons. Tricks sometimes backfire.

These two tricksters are well matched. Right from the beginning, they use tricks and cunning to try to outsmart each other. Loki shape-shifts into an old woman who pretends that she is lost. When Anansi comes close, Loki draws a dagger, but Anansi changes into a wolf and pretends that he is Loki's son Fenrir, and Loki does not strike. Next, Loki turns into a fly, a disguise he uses often. Anansi turns into a spider and tries to catch the fly in his web. When this doesn't work, Anansi changes back into a human and catches the fly in a jar. Furious, Loki turns back into a giant and smashes his way out of the jar.

Eventually, as night begins to fall, Loki hides from Anansi by disguising himself as a blade of grass. In the fading light, Anansi cannot find him, so he sets the grass on fire. But Loki is one step ahead. He uses this opportunity to escape the gods' watchful gaze and, disguised as a cloud, drifts away from the battlefield. Anansi wins by default.

**STATS**
# LOKI
AKA Loptr

**STRENGTHS:** Dangerous shape-shifter with great cunning. Has three monstrous children. Uses Viking weapons. Built like a giant.

**WEAKNESSES:** Jealousy. Not liked by the gods. Not good at keeping secrets.

**WINNER: ANANSI**

# PROFILE: **MALSUM**

The Algonquins are a Native American people from the northeastern United States and Canada. They have many myths and legends about the gods and spirits that they believed ruled over nature and the world. Among these are stories of twin brothers named Malsum and Glooskap, who were the sons of the Earth Mother.

*The Algonquins are a Native American people from northeastern North America.*

## Twin Brothers

Glooskap was good and wise but Malsum was evil and destructive. Malsum grew tired of his brother and plotted against him. When he found out that Glooskap could be killed only by an owl feather, he shot him with an owl-feather dart. But Glooskap came back to life, ready to take his revenge and rid the world of evil.

He called Malsum to a stream, pretending that a flowering reed could kill him. When Malsum arrived, Glooskap pulled up a fern and threw it at his brother—it was the only way he could be destroyed.

*Malsum became a wolf spirit that still sometimes comes out at night to hunt.*

# PROFILE: **SET**

Set was the ancient Egyptian god of deserts, storms, and chaos. He was the son of Nut, the sky goddess, and Geb, the god of the earth. In art, Set is shown as having a part-donkey, part-jackal head. Although, in some myths, he was seen as a hero, he also fought violently with his brother Osiris, and his nephew Horus.

## Set and Ra

Every night, Ra, the sun god, sailed through the underworld on his barge, accompanied by Set. On the journey, the boat was frequently attacked by the monstrous serpent, Apep. Every night, Set would spear the serpent while Ra cut off its head. Then the sun could rise again.

*Set killed his brother Osiris, then fought with Horus, Osiris's son, for the throne.*

## Set and Osiris

Osiris and his wife, Isis, once ruled Egypt. They were wise and well loved, but their brother, Set, was jealous. He tricked Osiris into climbing into a beautiful wooden chest, which he then sealed and threw into the Nile River. After many adventures, Isis found Osiris's body, but Set cut it into pieces and scattered it over Egypt. Isis gathered up the pieces and brought Osiris back to life. Set tried to take his revenge on Horus, Osiris's son, but Horus defeated him and exiled him to the desert.

*Set's head was a combination of a donkey's and a jackal's.*

*Set (left) and Horus (right) fought many battles, including a race in ships made of stone.*

# FIGHT 5: MALSUM VS. SET

The setting for tonight's fight is a bank of the Nile River, near Memphis in ancient Egypt. Two violent and ruthless gods of chaos and destruction—Malsum and Set—eye each other up as they prepare to do battle. Set has chosen the venue and has the advantage of being on his home ground. Malsum has chosen the fight time. He hates daylight, so he has picked an early evening start, when he can use his wolflike cunning. Unfortunately, he has not counted on this also being the very time that Set is at his most accurate with his spear.

## STATS
## MALSUM
### AKA Molsem, Malsumis

**STRENGTHS:** Can create poisonous creatures and plants. Has the cunning and stealth of a wolf.

**WEAKNESSES:** Fears daylight. Can be killed by the root of a fern plant.

The fight begins. At first Malsum manages to parry Set's spear throws with expert use of his ax. But Set has fought much more slippery opponents than this. He shape-shifts into a hippo and disappears into the river. When Malsum tries to follow him, Set suddenly rears his huge head and smashes Malsum's boat to pieces. But Malsum isn't finished yet and remembers the owl-feather trick that worked so well on his brother. While Set hauls himself out of the water, Malsum takes a dart from his holder and fires it at the god. Seth looks down scornfully and pulls out the dart. To Malsum's dismay, he is unharmed.

Daylight is beginning to break, and Malsum decides to make a hasty retreat back to the safety of the underworld. But as he starts to slink away, he feels something hard and heavy hit him in the back. Set has dug up a fern root and hurled it at the retreating god, not realizing that it was the only thing that could kill his opponent.

**WINNER: SET**

STATS
# SET
AKA Seth, Sheth, Setan, Seteh

STRENGTHS: Chief god. Killer of gods and giant serpents.

WEAKNESSES: Can be defeated by other gods, such as Horus.

# PROFILE: **THOR**

One of the most popular figures in Norse mythology, Thor was a larger-than-life character. Huge and strong, with a wild beard and hair, he loved fighting and feasting. He was god of thunder and law and order and also defender of Asgard against the giants.

## God of Thunder

Thor raced across the sky in a great chariot pulled by two giant goats. It was the sound of the goats' hooves that people heard as thunder. He was said to be able to summon storms by blowing through his beard. Thor wore a belt that doubled his strength and iron gauntlets that allowed him to grip any weapon. But his most famous weapon was his hammer, Mjollnir, which returned to Thor's hand after every throw.

*Thor doing battle from his chariot, which is pulled by giant goats.*

*Thor's many exploits included battling the monstrous serpent Jormungand. The two were fated to kill each other at Ragnarok.*

*(Left) Thor's hammer, Mjollnir, always hit its target and was strong enough to knock down a mountain. It was made for Thor by the dwarves.*

# PROFILE: **ARES**

Ares, the ancient Greek god of war, was the son of Zeus. Although admired for his great courage in battle, he was unpopular because he enjoyed violence and bloodshed for their own sake. He was known to rush into battle, regardless of who was right or wrong and would even change sides at will. The *Iliad*, a Greek epic poem, tells how Ares fought for the Trojans against the Greeks in the Trojan War. Badly wounded, he rode back to Mount Olympus, where he was healed by Zeus.

*Ares rode into battle on a chariot pulled by four horses.*

## Family Feuds

Ares' jealous and violent nature regularly got him into trouble. Myths tell how he fell in love with the goddess Aphrodite, who was married to his brother. When Aphrodite had an affair with Adonis, Ares was so jealous that he turned into a boar and killed him. Another time, Ares was tried for murder after killing his cousin, though he was later acquitted. The trial took place on a hill in Athens that later became the site for all murder trials.

*Ares wore bronze armor in battle and brandished a spear. In Roman mythology, he was known as Mars.*

*Aphrodite was the goddess of love. She and Ares had several children together.*

# FIGHT 6: THOR VS. ARES

Somewhere in the heavens, two of the true heavyweights of the gods get embroiled in a fight that should never have happened. Headstrong Ares, Greek god of war, hears Thor's goat-drawn chariot approaching and, in a moment of madness, complains about the noise. Thor is known for his quick temper and doesn't take this lightly. Swinging around, he taunts Ares by calling him a coward for being beaten in a fight by his sister Athena.

## STATS
## THOR
### AKA Donar

**STRENGTHS:** Magical belt and gauntlets that double his strength. Magical hammer that can crush mountains. Immensely strong and enjoys fighting.

**WEAKNESSES:** Can be tricked. Sometimes loses his hammer. Will be killed at Ragnarok

## STATS
## ARES
### AKA Mars (Roman)

**STRENGTHS:** A brave warrior. Immortal. Can shape-shift.

**WEAKNESSES:** Violent and bloodthirsty. Unreliable. Can be outwitted by giants, mortals, and other gods.

Ares sees red. He hurls his spear at the thunder god, but it misses. Then he charges in with his sword. Realizing that he has a fight on his hands, Thor straps on his magic belt and gauntlets and takes a firm grip on his hammer. He is not unduly worried by his bloodthirsty opponent. After all, he is used to fighting giants and sea monsters. But Ares plays his trump card, turns into a wild boar, and gores Thor in the leg. Furious, Thor raises his hammer, takes aim, and throws. The hammer never misses the mark and hits the boar with full force. Resuming his human shape, Ares has no option but to return to Mount Olympus to recover from his wounds.

**WINNER: THOR**

# CREATE YOUR OWN FIGHT

You might not agree with some of the fight results in this book. If that's the case, try writing your own fight report based on the facts supplied on the prefight profile pages. Better still, choose your own gods and goddesses and create your own fight.

## Monster Research

Once you have chosen your two gods or goddesses, do some research about them using books or the Internet. You can make them fairly similar, such as Odin and Zeus, or quite different, like Durga and the Morrigan.

## Stats Boxes

Think about stats for each god or goddess. Find out about any other names for the AKA section. Make a list of strengths, such as how powerful they are, and if they have the ability to shape-shift or use secret weapons. Also list any weaknesses.

## In the Ring

Pick a setting where your gods and goddesses are likely to meet, and write a blow-by-blow account of how you imagine the fight might happen. Think about each contestant's key characteristics, along with his or her strengths and weaknesses. Remember, there doesn't always have to be a winner.

## Gods and Goddesses

Here is a list of some other gods and goddesses who might want to join the Monster Fight Club:

Anubis
Apollo
Athena
Cupid
Diana
Frigg
Hel
Horus
Poseidon
Quetzalcoatl
Ra
Sekhmet
Sobek
Venus
Vulcan
Wakan Tanka

*Athena often got involved in the disputes of mortals.*

# GLOSSARY

**acquitted** (uh-KWIT-ed)
Found not guilty of a crime.

**Asgard** (AS-gahrd)
The name given to the world in which the Norsemen believed that their gods and goddesses lived.

**barge** (BARJ)
A long boat, often highly decorated.

**codex** (KOH-deks)
An ancient book or manuscript.

**defeating** (dih-FEET-ing)
Beating someone in a game or battle.

**Cyclops** (SY-klops)
A one-eyed giant in ancient Greek mythology.

**gauntlets** (GAWNT-lets)
Heavy leather gloves.

**immortal** (ih-MAWR-tul)
Never dying but living forever.

**legend** (LEH-jend)
Stories that are often based on events that are supposedly historical.

**mortal** (MOR-tul)
Being human and, therefore, not living forever.

**mythology** (mih-THAH-luh-jee)
A collection of myths, or traditional stories, that use supernatural characters to explain human behavior and natural events.

**Norse** (NAWRS)
Referring to the myths, beliefs, and lives of the Norsemen, or Vikings, who lived in Scandinavia in ancient times.

**nymphs** (NIMFS)
Spirits of nature in ancient Greek mythology who often appeared as beautiful young women.

**obsidian** (ub-SIH-dee-un)
A dark, glassy rock formed from volcanoes.

**Olympus** (uh-LIM-pus)
In ancient Greek mythology, Mount Olympus was believed to be the home of the gods.

**omen** (OH-men)
A sign, said to be from the gods, that warned of good or evil to come.

**reputation** (reh-pyoo-TAY-shun)
The ideas people have about another person, an animal, or an object.

**shape-shift** (SHAYP-shift)
Magically change shape from a human into an animal, or from animal to animal.

**Titans** (TY-tunz)
Giants in ancient Greek mythology, who were the ancestors of the Olympian gods and once ruled the world.

**violent** (VY-lent)
Strong, rough force.

# INDEX

## Web Sites

Due to the changing nature of Internet links, PowerKids Press has developed an online list of Web sites related to the subject of this book. This site is updated regularly. Please use this link to access the list:
www.powerkidslinks.com/mfc/gods/